W0081517

Rachel Carson's Wonder-Filled World

How the Scientist, Writer, and Nature Lover Changed the Environmental Movement

Kate Hannigan

Illustrated by **Katie Hickey**

CALKINS CREEK
AN IMPRINT OF ASTRA BOOKS FOR YOUNG READERS
New York

"Would you help me search for a fairy cave
on an August moon and a low, low tide?
I would love to try once more,
for the memories are precious."

To Rachel Carson, nature is a fairyland of birdsong and wildflowers, foxes and bees.

Ambling through the woods near her family's farm outside Pittsburgh, Pennsylvania, Rachel rarely sets off without her trusty companions— Mother, dog, and notebook.

"If I had influence with the good fairy who is supposed to preside over the christening of all children, I should ask that her gift to each child in the world be a sense of wonder so indestructible that it would last throughout life."

Using all her senses, Rachel . . .

sees busy bugs as big and beautiful as tigers,

hears a symphony of cardinals
and chickadees,

smells woodsmoke on the wind from nearby farms,

feels the spongy carpet of moss beneath her feet,

tastes plump, wild blueberries that line her path.

Rachel turns her adventures into stories. Some are good enough to publish in a magazine! When she leaves for college, Rachel dreams of becoming an author.

"My Favorite Recreation"
by Rachel Louise Carson (age 14)
"The sun was barely an hour
high when Pal and I set off for a
day of our favorite sport with a
lunch-box, a canteen, a note-book,
and a camera."

—St. Nicholas: An Illustrated
Magazine for Boys and Girls, July 1922

"Butterfly poised on a thistle's down.
Lend me your wings for a summer's day . . ."
—poem, school assignment, 1927

"Science is part of the reality of living; it is the what, the how, and the why of everything in our experience."

In Miss Skinker's science class, Rachel learns to use a microscope, slides, test tubes, and beakers. Rachel's love of nature blossoms under her teacher's encouragement. So Rachel decides to major in a subject not typical for women of the time: biology.

She graduates from college with top honors! When summer comes, Rachel takes Miss Skinker's advice to leave Pennsylvania and study at a biology laboratory along the Atlantic Coast. For the first time in her life, Rachel . . .

sees the majesty of the vast, churning ocean,
hears the power of the crashing waves,
smells the fishy fragrance on the breeze,
feels her feet sink into the sandy shoreline,
tastes the salty spray of the sea mist.

"I seem to have been born with a fascination for the ocean. For years before I had ever seen it, I thought about it and dreamed about it and tried to picture what it would be like."

In the autumn, Rachel moves to Baltimore for more schooling. But banks begin failing. Jobs disappear. The world sinks into an economic crisis called the Great Depression.

Rachel's family moves in, but often she's the only one earning a paycheck. Before she can finish studies to become "Dr. Carson," the money is spent. Rachel has to drop out.

Despite the hard times, Rachel finds work writing radio scripts for the Bureau of Fisheries and selling freelance articles to newspapers. Using vivid language, Rachel explains the habits of marine animals like turtles, fish, and ducks.

"Giant bluefin tuna, the speed of torpedoes and the strength of tigers in their streamlined bodies, are keeping a rendezvous this weekend off the rocky shores of Nova Scotia."

—The Baltimore Sun, August 28, 1938

With the mind of a scientist and the heart of a poet, Rachel asks readers to look at ocean life through the eyes of sea creatures—like dolphins, sponges, and starfish. Her essay in a national magazine becomes so popular, editors ask her to turn it into a book!

"The little fishes of the cove poured in restless shoals. The shining green and silver caravans wound in and out, swerving, diverging, and merging again, or at a sudden fright darting away like a shower of silver meteors."

—Under the Sea-Wind, 1941

After World War II, the Fish and Wildlife Service sends Rachel around the country to research the National Wildlife Refuge System.

She grows as a scientist, studying issues like habitat loss, pollution, and conservation, as well as learning about animals in danger of disappearing, like whooping cranes and trumpeter swans.

Ordinarily soft-spoken and bookish, Rachel wades through marshes, sails on ships, even plunges underwater to see the wonders of nature!

She grows as an author, too. Her fingers fly as she writes her second and third books, explaining the mysteries of the sea and complicated concepts like ecology. As she learns about pesticides and chemicals developed since the war, Rachel worries about the role humans play in helping—or harming—nature's balance.

"Fish, amphibian, and reptile, warm-blooded bird and mammal—each of us carries in our veins a salty stream in which the elements . . . are combined in almost the same proportions as in sea water."
—The Sea Around Us, 1951

"Almost every container of sea water that I bring up from the shore is flecked with white semitransparent objects, gossamer-fine, like the discarded garments of some very small fairy creature."

—*The Edge of the Sea, 1955*

Her books become best sellers!
Rachel leaves her job so she can write
full-time, building a cottage in Maine
on the edge of the Atlantic.

With her niece's little boy, she explores tide pools and trails. Even though she's grown up, Rachel still sees nature as a fairyland filled with birdsong and wildflowers, foxes and bees—even an "insect orchestra" serenading her at night.

"Most haunting of all is one I call the fairy bell ringer. I have never found him. I'm not sure I want to . . . It is exactly the sound that should come from a bell held in the hand of the tiniest elf . . ."

But walking with Roger amid tiny seedlings and tall spruce, Rachel knows nature is as fragile as a robin's egg. All around her, she . . .

sees trees cut down and buildings going up,
hears the honking of more drivers on the road,
smells the spray of weed killers and pesticides,
feels the sun's heat where shade used to be,
tastes the worry over what is to come.

Rachel wants to protect the beauty of nature—for Roger and for all children. Her concerns mount when a friend's letter arrives. She reads how chemicals meant to kill bugs are sprayed recklessly over towns and fields and forests. And humans!

She worries that birds are falling silent, wildflowers are turning brown, foxes and bees are dying off.

"The mosquito control plane flew over our small town last summer. . . . The 'harmless' shower bath killed seven of our lovely songbirds outright."
—letter from Olga Owens Huckins, January 1958

Rachel returns to her typewriter. Only now her heart beats with a new purpose: to INFORM and to INSPIRE. She reaches out to scientists and experts, to naturalists and biologists and zoologists, and most importantly to everyday people. The more Rachel learns, the more she believes chemical pesticides threaten nature's balance.

But headaches slow her down. Some days Rachel feels too weak to walk. What if time runs out before she can finish her book?

When Rachel types the last page, she looks
out to the ocean and . . .

sees razorbills dip and dive into the waves,
hears the singing of wood thrushes and warblers,
smells the sweetness of lavender buzzing with bees,
feels the soft breeze brush her tired eyes,
tastes the salt of her grateful tears.

"If I didn't at least try I could never again be happy in nature. But now I believe I have at least helped a little."

"A great woman has awakened the Nation by her forceful account of the dangers around us. We owe much to Rachel Carson." —Secretary of the Interior—
Stewart Udall, 1963

Warning about a world without birdsong, Rachel calls her book *Silent Spring*.

It is anything but quiet.

SILENT SPRING

BOSTON GLOBE

May 17th 1963

President Kennedy's Science Advisory Committee's report on dangers in misuse of pesticides reinforces the warnings given in Rachel Carson's 'Silent Spring'.

SPRING HAS SPRUNG

India Ink

LOS ANGE

SEPTEMBER 23rd 1962

NOT SO SILENT SPRING

A little book so explo
on every page that it
can hardly fail to
startle and frighten al
laymen who read it,
convulse the chemical
industry and possibly
create a whole new
political issue

— Eric Sevareid

"EVERY ONCE IN A WHILE IN THE HISTORY OF MANKIND, A BOOK HAS APPEARED WHICH HAS SUBSTANTIALLY ALTERED THE COURSE OF HISTORY."

— Senator Ernest Gruening
Alaska, 1963

Rachel Carson was called before a Senate subcommittee in 1963, months after publication of her book *Silent Spring*, which raised concerns about the harm done to the environment by the spraying of synthetic pesticides.

Author's Note

Published on September 27, 1962, Rachel Carson's *Silent Spring* captured the attention of backyard gardeners, birdwatching enthusiasts, heartland farmers, and even chemical company executives.

Holding tight to the sense of wonder she developed as a child in the woods, shy and unassuming Carson used her gift as a writer to awaken an emotional response to nature. She hoped *Silent Spring* might inspire readers to take action to protect the natural world she loved so dearly. Weaving together scientific concepts and poetic imagery, she sounded an alarm to the ways chemical pesticides such as DDT (short for dichlorodiphenyltrichloroethane) not only killed bugs but also the animals that ate them, entering the food chain in an interconnected "web of life" that ultimately threatened the health of children and adults.

Silent Spring did more than inform and inspire. It ignited a revolution.

"It is, in the deepest sense, a privilege as well as a duty to have the opportunity to speak out—to many thousands of people—on something so important."

Carson battled breast cancer and a host of other health ailments over the four years it took her to research and write *Silent Spring.* She often was afraid she would die before completing the project. But chapter after chapter, she pushed through the pain—a pain that sometimes left her needing a wheelchair. She told few friends she was sick.

Not everyone liked *Silent Spring.* The book angered some people, who dismissed it with personal insults against Carson, calling her "hysterical," "emotional," "a woman who loved cats," and "a spinster." She ignored the name-calling and instead kept focused on scientific facts, pointing to the misuse and overuse of pesticides.

Immediately after its publication, *Silent Spring* rocketed to the top of the bestseller lists and is considered the launching point of the modern environmental movement. Carson was called to Washington, DC, to testify before a congressional committee, and the government ordered a review of pesticide policy which ultimately led to the banning of some chemicals.

Carson died just eighteen months after *Silent Spring* was published. She didn't live to see the impact of her work, which still resonates today, or to hear the *good* names people called her—like "mother of the environmental movement." Her book laid the groundwork for many efforts to protect the earth: the Clean Air Act of 1963, the Wilderness Act of 1964, the National Environmental Policy Act of 1969, and the launching of the Environmental Protection Agency, as well as Earth Day in 1970. The Clean Water Act came in 1972 and the Endangered Species Act in 1973. In 1980, Rachel Carson was posthumously awarded the Presidential Medal of Freedom—the highest civilian honor in the United States—by President Jimmy Carter.

"We must all have a great sense of responsibility, and not let things happen because everyone takes the comfortable view that someone else is looking after it. Someone else isn't looking after it. It is your responsibility—yours and everyone else's."

Timeline

1907: Rachel Louise Carson is born on May 27 in Springdale, Pennsylvania.

1917: April, United States enters World War I.

1918: At age 10, publishes in a national children's magazine called *St. Nicholas*.

1925: Graduates Parnassus High School in Kensington, Pennsylvania.

1925–29: Attends Pennsylvania College for Women (now Chatham University) in Pittsburgh and studies under biology teacher and naturalist Mary Scott Skinker.

1929: Wins summer fellowship to study at the Marine Biological Laboratory in Woods Hole, Massachusetts; returns again over the years.

1929: Stock market crashes in October, ushering in 10-year Great Depression.

1929–1932: Wins scholarship to study at Johns Hopkins University, earns a master's degree in zoology; takes teaching jobs to help support family.

1934: Drops out of Hopkins' doctoral-degree program due to lack of funds.

1935: Father dies, leaving Carson to support entire family.

As a girl, Rachel Carson loved to take walks in the woods with her dog. She would bring along her mother too, as well as a notebook for writing down her observations.

1936: Takes job as aquatic biologist with the U.S. Bureau of Fisheries.

1937: Sister Marian dies, leaving Carson to raise her two nieces.

1941: November: Publishes *Under the Sea-Wind*, about birds and sea creatures along the eastern coast of North America; considered a definitive work of American nature writing.

1941: December: United States enters World War II.

1946–1948: Travels to collect data and write about the National Wildlife Refuge System.

1950: Learns she has breast cancer; tumor removed.

1951: Publishes *The Sea Around Us* about the world's oceans; it tops the best-seller list.

1952: Wins both the John Burroughs Medal for nature writing and the National Book Award for nonfiction for *The Sea Around Us*.

1953: Builds cottage she calls Silverledges on Boothbay Harbor in Maine.

1955: Publishes third book, *The Edge of the Sea*, about the ecology of the Atlantic Coast.

1956: Writes about adventures in nature with grandnephew Roger Christie for the magazine *Woman's Home Companion*, later published in 1965 as a book, *The Sense of Wonder*.

1957: Adopts Roger after niece dies.

1958: Her mother, Maria, dies.

1960: Undergoes surgery again for breast cancer.

1962: Publishes fourth book on September 27, *Silent Spring*, challenging widespread use of chemical pesticides like DDT.

1963: Testifies before Congress on June 4 about the dangers of pesticides.

1964: Rachel Carson dies at age 57 on April 14.

1970: U.S. Fish & Wildlife Service (formerly the U.S. Bureau of Fisheries) renames a coastal wildlife refuge near her Maine home the Rachel Carson National Wildlife Refuge.

1970: President Nixon establishes the Environmental Protection Agency to address the growing public demand for cleaner water, air, and land.

1972: Use of chemical pesticide DDT is banned.

Nature's Balance and the Web of Life

"The earth's vegetation is part of a web of life in which there are intimate and essential relations between plants and the earth, between plants and other plants, between plants and animals. Sometimes we have no choice but to disturb these relationships, but we should do so thoughtfully, with full awareness that what we do may have consequences remote in time and place."
—Rachel Carson in *Silent Spring*

DDT and the Web of Life

When we introduce pesticides, we impact every aspect of the web of life. Here is how DDT use brought about a decline in the population of birds like eagles, ospreys, robins, peregrine falcons, brown pelicans, and others during the 1960s, leading Rachel Carson to sound the alarm in *Silent Spring*.

- DDT is sprayed on crops and towns to control pests and mosquitoes.
- Rain washes DDT into streams, rivers, and lakes.
- Plants and animals living there absorb the DDT.
- Fish eat those plants and animals.
- Birds eat the fish.
- Female birds lay eggs, but the DDT in their systems disrupts calcium production, so eggshells crack and break in the nests before baby birds can hatch.
- Bird populations plummet.

Source: U.S. Fish & Wildlife Service

Words to Know

biology: The scientific study of life and living organisms.
conservation: The management of natural resources like water, trees, or bird population.
ecology: The branch of biology that studies the ways that organisms relate to each other and to their surroundings.
ecosystem: A community of organisms interacting within a specific environment.

habitat loss: When an ecosystem no longer provides protection or food needed for organisms to survive.
pesticides: Substances that are meant to repel, destroy, or control pests.
pollution: When contaminants like chemicals, light, or noise are introduced into an environment and cause harmful effects.

Ecologist? Zoologist? What Are You?

Rachel Carson loved to read books and write, almost as much as she loved to explore the woods and the ocean's shoreline. When she became an adult, she was able to merge these interests as a professional nature writer. In her lifetime, she made an impact in the biological sciences and beyond. Maybe YOU will grow up to wear one of the many different hats Rachel wore:

author: writes books or articles.
biologist: studies the science of living organisms.
conservationist: protects and preserves wildlife and the environment.
ecologist: studies the relationship of organisms to each other and their surroundings.
environmentalist: advocates for the protection of the natural world.
marine biologist: studies the organisms of the sea.
naturalist: studies and observes animals and plants.
zoologist: studies the behavior, classification, evolution, and other aspects of animals.

You Can Be a Naturalist Like Rachel Carson

"Many children, perhaps because they themselves are small and closer to the ground than we, notice and delight in the small and inconspicuous."

PUT TOGETHER YOUR OWN NATURE NOTEBOOK
You'll need paper, pencil, markers, or colored pencils.

MAKE OBSERVATIONS
Record what you discover, including details like what, where, and when.

TAKE TIME TO WONDER
Rachel Carson used the five senses when she engaged with nature.
- *See* all the colors in flowers, leaves, grasses, sky.
- *Hear* birdsong, water, wind through the trees.
- *Smell* the fragrance of flowers, the air just before a storm.
- *Feel* fuzzy moss growing on bark, slippery slime on rocks.
- *Taste* falling raindrops, snowflakes.

GATHER DATA
Sketch your nature observations, write descriptions. Collect small items, preserve them on your pages. Take photographs.

SHARE YOUR FINDINGS
Compare with classmates and friends.

Acknowledgments

Grateful thanks to Professor Mark Madison, historian for the U.S. Fish & Wildlife Service and educator with the National Conservation Training Center. Thanks to the late Frances Collin, Sarah Yake, and the Estate of Rachel Carson. And to husband-and-wife science teachers Tony and Deb Del Campo, lovers of nature, biology, and America's public lands, and inspirations to countless lucky learners.

Rachel Carson conducted U.S. Fish and Wildlife Service field research in 1952 in the Florida Keys with her colleague Bob Hines. Trained as a marine biologist, she merged her interests in science, nature, and poetry to write award-winning books about the ocean before her most important work, *Silent Spring*.

Bibliography

All quotations used in the book can be found in the following sources marked with an asterisk (*).

MAGAZINE AND NEWSPAPER ARTICLES
*Carson, Rachel Louise (age 14). "My Favorite Recreation." *St. Nicholas: An Illustrated Magazine for Boys and Girls*, May–October 1922.

*Carson, R. L. "Giants Of The Tide Rip Off Nova Scotia Again." *Baltimore Sun,* August 28, 1938.

*Lewine, Frances. "Gentle Gal Pens Scathing Indictment On Indiscriminate Use of Pesticides." The *Daily Record* (Long Branch, NJ), September 28, 1962.

*Raleigh [WV] *Register*. "New Pesticide Research Lab May Halt 'Silent Spring.'" May 8, 1963.

BOOKS
*Carson, Rachel. *Under the Sea-Wind.* New York: Oxford University Press, 1941.

*——. *The Sea around Us.* New York: Oxford University Press, 1951.

*——. *The Edge of the Sea.* Boston: Houghton Mifflin, 1955.

*——. *Silent Spring.* Boston: Houghton Mifflin, 1962.

*——. *The Sense of Wonder.* New York: Harper & Row, 1965.

*——. *Lost Woods: The Discovered Writing of Rachel Carson.* Edited by Linda Lear. Boston: Beacon Press, 1998.

*Lear, Linda. *Rachel Carson: Witness for Nature.* New York: Henry Holt, 1997.

*Matthiessen, Peter, ed. *Courage for the Earth: Writers, Scientists, and Activities Celebrate the Life and Writing of Rachel Carson.* Boston: Houghton Mifflin, 2007.

Lawlor, Laurie. *Rachel Carson and Her Book That Changed the World.* Illustrated by Laura Beingessner. New York: Holiday House, 2014.

WEBSITES**
*American Chemical Society. "Legacy of Rachel Carson's Silent Spring." acs.org/education/whatischemistry/landmarks/rachel-carson-silent-spring.html.

Lear, Linda. The Life and Legacy of Rachel Carson. RachelCarson.org.

Rachel Carson Homestead. RachelCarsonHomestead.org.

U.S. Fish & Wildlife Service. Rachel Carson National Wildlife Refuge. fws.gov/refuge/rachel-carson.

**Websites active at time of publication

For Olivia Issa, who also has a keen sense of wonder —*Kate*

For Mandy, who saw the wonder in everything—x —*Katie*

Picture Credits

Library of Congress, 94505448: 36; Rachel Carson Papers, Yale Collection of American Literature, Beinecke Rare Book and Manuscript Library, Yale University, used by permission: 37; U.S. Fish and Wildlife Service: 38.

Text Credits

Rachel Carson books (see bibliography) are reprinted by permission of Frances Collin, Trustee.

Text copyright © 2025 by Kate Hannigan
Illustrations copyright © 2025 by Katie Hickey
All rights reserved. Copying or digitizing this book for storage, display, or distribution in any other medium is strictly prohibited.

For information about permission to reproduce selections from this book, please contact permissions@astrapublishinghouse.com.

Calkins Creek
An imprint of Astra Books for Young Readers,
a division of Astra Publishing House
astrapublishinghouse.com
Printed in China

ISBN: 978-1-6626-8057-1 (hc)
ISBN: 978-1-6626-8058-8 (eBook)
Library of Congress Control Number: 2024932308

First edition

10 9 8 7 6 5 4 3 2 1

Design by Barbara Grzeslo
The text is set in Calibri.
The illustrations are done in watercolor pencil, gouache, and Procreate.